Value a Stock

Mariusz Skonieczny

Investment Publishing

Mariusz Skonieczny/Investment Publishing
1202 Far Pond Cir
Mishawaka, IN 46544
www.classicvalueinvestors.com

Ordering Information:
Quantity sales. Special discounts are available on quantity purchases by corporations, associations, and others. For details, contact the "Special Sales Department" at the address above.

How to Value a Stock/ Mariusz Skonieczny. —1st ed.
ISBN 978-0-9848490-7-9

Table of Contents

Introduction

Over the years of communicating with various investors, I have seen that there is a desire to learn how to value companies in order to make informed investment decisions. As with everything that I write, I want to explain concepts in easy-to-understand terms. I think that too many experts are so wrapped up in their fields that they can no longer communicate with someone on a lower level. I see this in all disciplines. Consequently, books written by experts tend to be extremely hard to understand unless you already have a strong foundation.

My goal for this book is to explain how to value companies in an easy-to-follow format. I will cover various valuation techniques because different methods are suitable for different companies. Hopefully, by the end, you will have enough understanding that you will tackle company valuations on your own and not be so dependent on analysts' price targets.

I am a value investor, which means that my goal is to buy the stock of a company for less than its value. However, in order to do that, I must know how to value companies.

The weird thing about value is that it differs depending on who is valuing it. This is true of literally anything that you can think of. How much is a particular car worth?

A) $1,000
B) $30,000
C) $5,000
D) it depends

The answer is D) it depends. If you ask a liquidator, he might value it at $1,000 because this is how much the parts are worth. If you ask a dealer, he would tell you $30,000 because this is how much money the car is selling for on the market.

You can have a similar situation with a business. You have a value as a going concern and you have a liquidation value. Let's say you own a restaurant. If you ask a liquidator, he would value it at a price that is equal to the value of the assets, such as the refrigerators, tables, and cooking equipment. If you ask a hedge fund manager, the value will be different, especially if the restaurant is profitable.

The value will be based on your restaurant's earning power.

In the world of business, no owner would be foolish enough to sell a perfectly good business for the value of its parts if the business is hugely profitable. However, if the business were losing money, then the situation would be different. In this case, it might make sense to sell it for the value of the parts but not much less than that. If the value of the restaurant equipment were $50,000, you wouldn't sell it for $1,000, right? It would not make any sense.

Well, this is in the private business world. In the public business world, anything is possible and I mean literally anything. This is because the players might be price insensitive. Money managers care more about total assets under management than the prices of particular securities. Consequently, you can have a company selling for a fraction of its liquidation value even when it is profitable.

CHAPTER 1

Liquidation Value

A liquidation value can be calculated for any business, whether it's profitable, marginally profitable, or unprofitable. Whether the market prices the company anywhere near the liquidation value is a different story. Businesses that are doing well should not be priced anywhere near the liquidation value because they are worth more alive than dead. However, this does not mean that you should not calculate the liquidation value anyway. It may serve as a margin of safety below which the stock price should not fall. For unprofitable businesses, the calculation of the liquidation value is more important because this is how much the business might be sold for if it were actually liquidated.

Liquidation value, as the name implies, is the amount of money that you can get if you liquidate all the assets of a business minus paying off all the debts. What is the liquidation value of a house? It is the sales price minus the mortgage. What is the liquidation value of a car? It is the sales price minus the loan. If you don't have a mortgage on a house or a loan on a car, then it is simply the sales price. Yes, I know there are other expenses like the realtor's fees and closing costs, but let's not complicate things here.

In order to estimate the liquidation value of a business, you need to first figure out what its assets are. A good place to start is the balance sheet. Notice that I said "a good place to start." Unfortunately, this is where most investors finish. They simply look at what the balance sheet says, and they go with it. This can lead to improper estimates. For example, inventory is an asset. Can all of the inventory be liquidated for what the balance sheet says? Absolutely not. The kind of inventory Home Depot has is completely different from the kind of inventory McDonald's has. Home Depot's inventory comprises finished goods, which can last for a long time. McDonald's inventory includes food products, which are perishable.

On the balance sheet, assets are listed in order of liquidity, meaning that cash is listed first and that property, plant, and equipment (PP&E) is listed last. Cash is the most liquid because it is the standard of liquidity and real estate or heavy machinery are the least liquid because it would take time to turn them into cash.

Current Assets	
Cash and cash equivalents	$X,XXX
Marketable securities	$X,XXX
Accounts receivable	$X,XXX
Inventories	$X,XXX
Pre-paid expenses	$X,XXX
Total Current Assets	$X,XXX
Marketable securities	$X,XXX
Property, plant, and equipment	$X,XXX
Other assets	$X,XXX
Total Assets	$X,XXX

CASH AND CASH EQUIVALENTS

When calculating the value of cash as part of the liquidation value, you usually want to assign it 100 percent of what the balance sheet says the value is. Make sure from the footnotes that this cash is not restricted in any way. For example, some companies may keep a portion of their cash offshore to avoid paying taxes, and if this cash were to be moved to the home country, it would be taxed. The liquidation value for such cash would not be 100 percent of what the balance sheet states.

MARKETABLE SECURITIES

When you as a person have surplus cash, you can either keep it as cash or park it in tradable financial assets, which can consist of stocks, bonds, or any other investment securities. Well, companies can do the same thing with their cash. When they do that, the amount can no longer be shown on the balance sheet as cash and instead must be shown as marketable securities. However, note that on the balance sheet, the marketable securities appear under current assets and non-current assets. They show up twice. This is because if the securities are anticipated to be converted into cash within one year, they are listed under current assets. If not, they are listed under non-current assets.

The estimation of the liquidation value of marketable securities is different depending on whether they are current assets or non-current assets. The marketable securities in the current assets section of the balance sheet are reported at current market values. This means that at the end of each quarter, they are reported at whatever levels they traded at on the last day of the quarter. Consequently, the liquidation value will not vary much from the reported amount, unless, of course, the securities are volatile. The marketable securities in the non-current section are not adjusted to market value. They are reported at cost. This means that if they were bought at $10 million and are currently trading at $5 million, they are reported on the balance sheet at $10 million. This is a big deal if you don't know that.

The knowledge of the composition of marketable securities will help you in estimating their liquidation value. Are they government bonds or corporate bonds? Government bonds are considered less risky, unless they are bonds from developing nations. What is the maturity of the bonds? The longer the maturity, the more they fluctuate in value with changes in interest rates. If they are corporate bonds, are the issuers still in business? Do the rating agencies consider these bonds risky? Are they stocks? If so, which stocks? Are the stocks volatile in price? Are they mutual funds? If so, which mutual funds?

One time, I was researching a company that had marketable securities in the form of a stock from another company. The company received the stock after it sold an asset to this other company. Within weeks, the price of this stock declined by 80 percent. If you didn't check the stock's price history when you were determining the liquidation value, you would never have known that the liquidation value was down by so much.

In summary, there is no magic formula when estimating the liquidation value of a company's marketable securities. You have to know what is in the portfolio. Marketable securities under current assets are likely to be valued very close to what the balance sheet says. But for marketable securities under non-current assets, the discrepancy between what is reported and the liquidation value can be large.

ACCOUNTS RECEIVABLE

Accounts receivable is the amount of money that the company's customers owe to the company. In a typical business-to-business transaction, a client receives a product or service and pays for it with terms typically of 30 to 60 days. The amount that is owed is the client's accounts payable and the company's accounts receivable.

Everybody loves a strict formula or a rule of thumb for calculating the liquidation value of accounts payable. When you actually think about it, it is challenging to do. For example, let's imagine that your friend buys a product from you for $1,000, and you let him pay you in 30 days. You have accounts receivable of $1,000. What is the liquidation value of the accounts receivable? It depends. Is your friend reliable? Does he have a job? Did he pay you back in the past? If the answer is no to these questions, the liquidation value of the accounts receivable is probably zero. However, if he is responsible, then the liquidation value might be 90 percent.

Notice that I did not say 100 percent. This is because if you wanted to quickly convert your accounts receivable into cash, you might have to use some kind of financing company that would buy the accounts receivable from you by giving you only $900 and collecting $1,000 from your friend. The $100 would be their profit for providing this service to you. This is referred to as "factoring," where a business sells its accounts receivable to a third-party commercial financing company, known as a "factor." The factoring company will pay anywhere from 80 to 95 percent of the face value, depending on the industry, client's credit history, and other criteria.

To properly estimate the liquidation value of accounts receivable, you have to think like a factor company. Who are the clients behind the accounts receivable? Are they creditworthy? Is the majority of the amount from one client? The risk factors in the 10-K will tell you if the company has a high customer concentration.

If the repayment probability of accounts receivable is high, then you can use a 5 to 20 percent discount when calculating the liquidation value. This is approximately how much a factor would shave off.

There are also quantitative tools that you can use to determine the health of the accounts receivable:

- Calculate the Accounts Receivable Turnover Ratio
- Calculate the Average Collection Period
- Analyze Allowance for Doubtful Accounts

ACCOUNTS RECEIVABLE TURNOVER RATIO

The accounts receivable turnover ratio is the number of times a business collects its average accounts receivable during a given period.

Accounts Receivable Turnover = Sales/Average Accounts Receivable

This ratio can be calculated for a quarter or a year. If it is calculated for a quarter, you use the sales for that quarter and the average accounts receivable for that quarter. If it is calculated for a year, then you use the sales for that year and the average accounts receivable for that year.

The average accounts receivable is derived by simply adding the amount of accounts receivable at the end of the reporting period to the amount of accounts receivable at the beginning of the reporting period and then dividing by 2.

Average Accounts Receivable = (End of Period A/R + Beginning of Period A/R)/2

To find the accounts receivable at the end of the period, you simply look at the balance sheet at the end of the period. To find the amount at the beginning, you look at the balance sheet amount from the prior period because the ending amount from the prior period is the beginning amount of the next period.

If you calculate the accounts receivable turnover ratios for several quarters and you notice that the turnover is deteriorating, then the quality of accounts receivable might be going down. If this is the case, then it is something you need to consider when estimating the accounts receivable liquidation value.

AVERAGE COLLECTION PERIOD

The average collection period measures the time that it takes for a business to collect its accounts receivables from its customers.

Average Collection Period = (Days x Average Accounts Receivable)/Sales

The days could be number of days in a quarter (90) or year (365).

If this number deteriorates (increases), then the quality of the accounts receivable might have gone down, which means that the liquidation value estimate should carry a bigger discount.

ALLOWANCE FOR DOUBTFUL ACCOUNTS

If you have ever run a business, you know that some accounts receivable will never be collected. This amount should be estimated and reported. Obviously, a healthy business only has a small portion of customers that don't pay. When reporting accounts receivable on the balance sheet, businesses have to estimate the allowance for doubtful accounts, which is a contra account to accounts receivable. The allowance for doubtful accounts could also be called the provision for doubtful accounts or the allowance for uncollectible accounts.

Accounts receivable	$1,000
Minus: Allowance for doubtful accounts	$50
Net, Accounts receivable	$950

On the balance sheet, companies will report either all these three lines or the net amount. Every time you see "net," you know that the allowance for doubtful accounts has already been applied. Then, to get the breakdown, you need to visit the footnotes.

The allowance for doubtful accounts is a loss to the business, so it has to be reported on the income statement as such. On the income statement, it is called a bad debt expense (BDE). So, the allowance for doubtful accounts shows up on the balance sheet while the bad debt expense shows up on the income statement. Both of them are the management's estimates. To analyze the quality of the accounts receivable, both of these estimates can be compared to the actual write-offs (WO).

Comparison Number 1: bad debt expense (BDE) to write-off (WO)

Ratio = BDE/WO

In the ideal world, this ratio would be 1 because the bad debt expense should have been estimated at exactly the amount that was later written off. Calculate this ratio for several years or quarters to see if the management is doing a good job at estimating it. The standard range should be around 1. If the ratio suddenly falls, it could mean that the write-offs soared and the company started experiencing problems collecting on their accounts receivable.

Comparison Number 2: beginning allowance for doubtful accounts (BADA) to write-offs

Ratio = BADA/WO

The idea behind this ratio is that the beginning allowance for doubtful accounts should have been enough to cover all the write-offs that happened during the year. Again, the ideal ratio is 1. But if the write-offs suddenly soar, then this ratio will fall, showing you that the company might be experiencing problems with collections.

In summary, in order to properly assess the liquidation value of the accounts receivable, you need to understand this asset well. Only then can you make an educated guess as to the amount of money for which it could be liquidated.

INVENTORY

In the normal course of business, when companies sell their products, they generate sales and deliver their products to their customers by releasing them from inventory. At that point, the inventory is sold or liquidated for more than what it is reported on the balance sheet because on the balance sheet, inventory is reported at cost. It has to be sold for more than the cost; otherwise, there would be no point in running a business.

However, if a company's inventory has to be liquidated as-is and fast, it might have to be sold below cost. The liquidation value depends on many factors. Is the inventory from a retailer or a manufacturer? If it is from a retailer, then the inventory will mostly consist of finished and ready-to-sell products (think Walmart). In this case, the inventory's value might actually be high. Remember that when retailers buy products, they buy them wholesale and then mark them up. For example, they might buy an item for $10 and resell it for $20. The inventory on the balance sheet would show $10 for that item. So, if the inventory were to be liquidated quickly, it might actually be sold for $15, which is still a discount off the retail price but 50 percent more than the cost of inventory. So, don't assume that the liquidation value of the inventory is always below cost. The amount of discount or premium would really depend on the type of product and the level of demand that exists in the marketplace.

If the inventory belongs to the manufacturer, then it has a completely different composition. A manufacturer's inventory is categorized into raw materials, work-in-progress or semi-finished goods, and finished goods.

If you are a shoe manufacturer, the leather, rubber for the soles, and thread are categorized as raw materials. If the raw materials are commodities, then they might be liquidated at only a slight discount from what you paid for them.

When you start cutting up the raw materials and assembling them, then the resulting semi-finished product, created from raw materials plus labor, becomes your work-in-progress inventory. It would be unfortunate if you had to liquidate your inventory at this point because you would not only lose the opportunity to sell your shoes at full price, but you probably wouldn't recoup the money you spent on raw materials and labor. So, overall, the work-in-progress inventory might have to be seriously discounted by maybe 70 percent.

Once your shoes are complete, they become part of the "finished goods" portion of the inventory. If they were to be liquidated at this point, you could get more money for them because they are finished. Again, depending on the product, you might actually do very well in terms of the liquidation price. If you have to go below the cost of the finished goods, you might still get 80 percent.

When estimating the liquidation value of a manufacturer's inventory, you should read the footnotes to determine the proportion of raw materials, work-in-progress goods, and finished goods in the inventory. Let's say that the total inventory is $900,000, as shown in the following example.

Raw materials	$300,000
Work-in-progress	$300,000
Finished goods	$300,000
Total inventory	$900,000

You estimate that the raw materials can be liquidated for 85 percent of their cost.

$300,000 x 85% = $255,000$

You estimate that the work-in-progress goods can be liquidated for 30 percent of their cost.

$300,000 x 30% = $90,000$

You estimate that the finished goods can be liquidated for 70 percent of their cost.

$300,000 x 70% = $210,000$

Based on that, your liquidation value of the total inventory would be $555,000, which is 62 percent of $900,000, the total inventory cost.

To be as accurate as possible with such a calculation, you need to know the business. You need to know the products, how they are made, what raw materials they need, and what they sell for in the marketplace.

PREPAID EXPENSES

Prepaid expenses are expenditures that have already been incurred for a benefit that the company will receive in the near future. Examples include advances for insurance policies, rent, and taxes. Unless you know that some of the money can be refunded, just assign it zero liquidation value.

PROPERTY, PLANT, AND EQUIPMENT

Property, plant, and equipment (PP&E) is a term that refers to all of the company's assets that are not intended to be sold to customers. They are referred to as "fixed assets" and they are used on a repeated basis to provide services or manufacture products. The most common fixed assets include land, buildings, machinery, furniture, and tools.

When a business is being liquidated, property, plant, and equipment can yield a significant amount of money. As with everything else, in order to properly estimate the liquidation value of property, plant, and equipment, you need to know the condition and quality of those assets.

On the balance sheet, the property, plant, and equipment expense is reported at cost. Then, every year the value is reduced by depreciation.

Property, plant, and equipment	$1,000
Accumulated depreciation	-$200
Property, plant, and equipment, net	$800

In everyday life, when we think of depreciation, we think of wear and tear. However, in accounting, this is not what depreciation means. Under Generally Accepted Accounting Principles (GAAP), revenues must be matched to costs. This means that costs can be expenses only when revenues are recorded. In order for businesses to make their products or provide their services, they use fixed assets, but those assets last for a long time. So, in accounting, instead of expensing the cost of a building or other fixed asset in one year, the cost is spread over many years through a depreciation expense. That quarterly or yearly depreciation expense on the income statement is added on the balance sheet to accumulated depreciation, a contra account to PP&E, which reduces its net value.

Because of this, the balance sheet value could be completely off from the market value. For example, cars are depreciated over five years. So, if you bought a new car for $10,000, this amount would be reported on the balance sheet as property, plant, and equipment. After one year, this is what the balance sheet entry would look like:

Property, plant, and equipment	$10,000
Accumulated depreciation	-$2,000
Property, plant, and equipment, net	$8,000

The balance sheet would show that your car is worth $8,000, but is this the case? I am sure that you have heard that a new car loses a lot of value the moment you drive it off the dealer's lot. So, your car is most likely worth less than what the balance sheet says it is worth after one year.

After five years, this is what the balance sheet entry would look like:

Property, plant, and equipment	$10,000
Accumulated depreciation	-$10,000
Property, plant, and equipment, net	$0

According to the balance sheet, your car is worth nothing. Again, this might be totally inaccurate. I bought a Honda Civic in 2003 when it was brand new and I drove it for 15 years. According to the balance sheet, it would have been worthless at the end of 2008. Clearly, the balance sheet value was wrong.

What about real estate? The balance sheet will show declining value from year to year while the property value could actually be increasing. However, the GAAP rules do not allow you to show such an increase.

The bottom line is this. Some fixed assets hold value better than other fixed assets, and you need to keep that in mind when calculating the liquidation value of property, plant, and equipment. If you are dealing with specialized equipment, then you might be able to liquidate it for only 20 percent of what the balance sheet says it is worth because the buyer pool is limited.

The only way to be accurate with the liquidation estimate of property, plant, and equipment is to study its composition and research the price each item could bring if all of it was liquidated. There is no way around it. There is no magic formula that works for every business.

OTHER ASSETS

So far, we discussed the liquidation value of tangible assets. Businesses also have intangible assets such as brand names, customer lists, and reputation. But because their value is difficult to quantify, we will ignore it and stick with the value of the tangible assets.

LIQUIDATION VALUE TEMPLATE

Now that you have an understanding of what it takes to estimate liquidation value, you can construct your own template based on the following example.

ASSETS	Balance Sheet		Liquidation Value
Current Assets			
Cash and cash equivalents	$10,000	100%	$10,000
Marketable securities	$5,000	100%	$5,000
Accounts receivable	$20,000	80%	$16,000
Inventories	$50,000	50%	$25,000
Pre-paid expenses	$10,000	0%	$0
Total Current Assets	$95,000		$56,000
Marketable securities	$1,000	80%	$800
Property, plant, and equipment	$100,000	15%	$15,000
Other assets	$50,000	0%	$0
Total Assets	$246,000		$71,800
LIABILITIES			
Current liabilities	$5,000	100%	$5,000
Debt	$10,000	100%	$10,000
Other liabilities	$2,000	100%	$2,000
Total liabilities	$17,000		$17,000
Liquidation Value			$54,800

Under the balance sheet column, enter the proper amounts straight from the latest balance sheet. Under the column with percentages, enter your estimate of the percentage of value that can be obtained in the event of liquidation.

Under liabilities, you need to enter all the liabilities at 100 percent because when the company liquidates, all the debts and outstanding balances have to be satisfied in full.

Finally, based on the amounts you enter, your valuation template should calculate the liquidation value for you, and you can compare it to the market cap of the company you are analyzing.

NET-NET LIQUIDATION VALUE

If you are familiar with value investing, you have probably heard of net-net investing, which was introduced by Benjamin Graham. This is a method of investing in stocks that trade below the net-net liquidation value. To calculate the net-net liquidation value, you take the liquidation value of the current assets (cash, marketable securities, accounts receivable, and inventory) and subtract all liabilities. You ignore the value of property, plant, and equipment.

SUMMARY

An estimate of the liquidation value is only good for a single point in time. It changes from day to day, quarter to quarter, and year to year, and has to be recalculated every time any of the numbers change. When it comes to unprofitable companies, the liquidation value tends to decline over time because to cover for losses, either cash has to be burned, assets have to be sold off, or debt has to be added to stay alive. Consequently, you need to figure out the cash burn and make sure that you buy the stock cheap enough in relation to the market cap so that the company has enough time to liquidate or return to profitability before the liquidation value falls below the price that you paid.

To calculate the cash burn, simply analyze the cash flow statement to see how much cash is being lost during each quarter or year. Also, don't just blindly follow the cash flow statement without knowing if the company did anything to limit the cash burn. Remember, financial statements only tell you the past. Often a phone call to the company will help you estimate the cash burn.

CHAPTER 2

Earnings and P/E Ratio

When entrepreneurs start businesses, they do so mainly for one reason – to make a profit. Yes, they might enjoy the activities required to service their clients, but at the end of the day, they must make money from the business in order for it to survive long term. Consequently, the value of a business is based on the amount of money that it generates for its owners.

The simplest way to value a profitable business is take the net income and multiply it by a certain earnings multiple, and you are done. For example, let's say that you have a business generating $1 million in revenues and $300,000 in net income.

Revenues	$1,000,000
Expenses	-$700,000
Net income	$300,000

To value it, you multiply $300,000 of net income times an earnings multiple of 10 to arrive at a value of $3 million. If this business were trading on the stock market for this amount, it would have a P/E ratio of 10. P/E ratio stands for price-to-earnings ratio. If this business had issued 100,000 shares, the $300,000 of net income would translate to $3 per share and the $3 million in value for the business would translate to $30 per share.

The problem that many investors have is they don't feel comfortable with choosing an adequate earnings multiple. Should it be 10, 20, 15, or 30? Obviously, picking the right earnings multiple matters because such a decision has a significant impact on the final estimate of value. I believe that the best way to deal with this issue is to take things back to the basics.

Imagine that your friend comes to you and asks you to buy his business, which has the same financials as in the last example, meaning $1 million in revenue and $300,000 in net income. Forget right now that you are trying to get a deal. He is your friend, so you pay him a fair price. Would you pay him 10 times earnings, 5 times earnings, or 50 times earnings?

At this point, there is too little information to make that determination.

- How reliable are the earnings?
- Is the business going to earn that much or more going forward?
- What did it earn during the prior years?
- Are the revenues, and thus the earnings, dependent on any particular large client that could leave after you buy the business?
- Is the business growing?
- If so, how fast is it growing?
- Does it have any debt?
- Is this debt coming due anytime soon?
- Is the interest on this debt about to increase?
- Are any capital expenditures needed in order to maintain the current earning power?
- Is the $300,000 in earnings before or after taxes?

It is just common sense that you would want to know the answers to such questions before making an offer. However, in the public markets, investors want you to give them a rule of thumb for what earnings multiples to use. Don't you think this is a bit naive? They don't know anything about the business, but they want to value it anyway.

The key to valuing a business in this simple way is to investigate the quality of the earnings – "E," and predict their direction. The earnings can grow, contract, stay the same, or fluctuate.

STABLE BUT NOT GROWING "E"

If the earnings are stable, but not growing, I like to use an earnings multiple of 10 when valuing a business. This means that I get my money back in 10 years and I get to keep the business afterwards.

GROWING "E"

If the earnings are stable and growing, then I will use a multiple of anything between 12 and 20. Whether I am closer to the bottom or top of the range will depend on the growth rate. Let me give you three growth scenarios for the next five years.

Scenario Number 1 – Earnings Growth at 10 percent

Year 0: EPS =	$1.00
Year 1: EPS =	$1.10
Year 2: EPS =	$1.21
Year 3: EPS =	$1.33
Year 4: EPS =	$1.46
Year 5: EPS =	$1.61

Based on this scenario, I don't want to value the stock at more than 12 times earnings or $12 per share. By Year 5, earnings are going to be $1.61 per share, so at that point, the stock price should be around $20 per share with a really conservative earnings multiple. If I pay $12 for it today, then I will almost double my money in five years. I am OK with that. But if I paid 17 times earnings, it would mean $17 per share. It is too much because I don't want to wait five years to go from $17 to $20 per share.

However, if the growth is 20 percent, then I can afford to pay more and still double my money in five years.

Scenario Number 2 – Earnings Growth at 20 percent

Year 0: EPS =	$1.00
Year 1: EPS =	$1.20
Year 2: EPS =	$1.44
Year 3: EPS =	$1.73
Year 4: EPS =	$2.07
Year 5: EPS =	$2.49

Based on this scenario, the company's stock will probably trade at $30 per share with $2.49 in earnings per share. Consequently, I can afford to pay $15 per share or 15 times earnings and still double my money in five years. If Mr. Market was pricing the stock at a P/E ratio of 12, it would be slightly undervalued based on my estimate of value.

Scenario Number 3 – Earnings Growth at 30 percent

Year 0: EPS =	$1.00
Year 1: EPS =	$1.30
Year 2: EPS =	$1.69
Year 3: EPS =	$2.20
Year 4: EPS =	$2.86
Year 5: EPS =	$3.71

Based on the third scenario, the company's stock will probably trade at $45 per share with $3.71 in earnings per share. Consequently, you can be more generous with the current valuation and pay 20 times earnings because from $20 per share, the stock would still be a double in five years. If the stock were trading at a P/E ratio of 12, it would be significantly undervalued. It would be a steal.

SUPER FAST GROWING "E"

In certain circumstances, businesses can see their earnings grow exponentially before they level off. This usually happens when businesses scale. For example, let's say you have a company with an infrastructure that can handle $10 million worth of business and produce a 30 percent net profit margin.

Revenues	$10,000,000
Expenses	-$7,000,000
Net income	$3,000,000

This is what the income statement would look like with $10 million in revenues. However, with only $7.1 million in revenues, the business would only generate $100,000 in net income because the expenses would still be at $7 million.

Revenues	$7,100,000
Expenses	-$7,000,000
Net income	$100,000

With each increase in revenues, net income would grow very quickly until it stabilized.

Revenues	$7,100,000	$7,500,000	$8,000,000	$8,500,000	$9,000,000	$9,500,000	$10,000,000
Expenses	$7,000,000	$7,000,000	$7,000,000	$7,000,000	$7,000,000	$7,000,000	$7,000,000
Net income	$100,000	$500,000	$1,000,000	$1,500,000	$2,000,000	$2,500,000	$3,000,000

Note that net income would go from $100,000 on $7.1 million in revenues to $3 million on $10 million in revenues. Such growth is possible because of operating leverage. In this case, I would not use this method of valuation because I would have to assign a ridiculously high earnings multiple to the current earnings. Instead, I would try to predict what the future earnings would be for expected revenue targets. This would allow me to predict the future stock price by multiplying the future earnings by a conservative earnings multiple (between 12 and 15). Then, I would compare it to the current stock price to see if the appreciation potential were high enough. I would completely ignore the current P/E ratio.

To determine whether the company has a business model that can benefit from operating leverage, you have to understand the cost structure and how it reacts to various revenue levels. Cost structures with high levels of fixed expenditures stay relatively constant when revenues increase. However, they also stay relatively constant when revenues fall, which can cause you to lose a lot of money.

FLUCTUATING "E"

Wall Street loves stocks that grow earnings year after year, but constant growth is unsustainable. It is normal for earnings to fluctuate from one year to another. Actually, for some cyclical industries, it would be suspicious if earnings grew in only a straight line. For example, oil service companies are extremely cyclical because their business activity depends on the price of oil, which is volatile.

Before you can value a company that has fluctuating earnings, you have to determine whether the earnings are fluctuating around some stable level, growing in a fluctuating way, or declining in a fluctuating way.

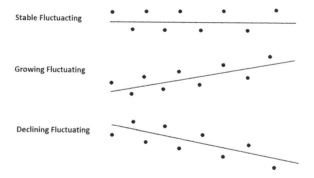

Once you determine the pattern of fluctuation, you can calculate some kind of normalized or average earnings instead of earnings from a particular year, which could be overstating or understating the earning power of a business. Then, you multiply your normalized earnings by an earnings multiple that was chosen based on the ideas described earlier.

CONTRACTING "E"

Unfortunately, there are companies that really are in decline. In order to value them, you need to know more information.

- How fast are earnings contracting?

- When will the decline stop, if ever?
- When the decline stops, what will the earnings be?
- After the decline stops, will growth resume?

The problem with declining earnings is that they may eventually turn into losses, and you cannot use an earnings multiple on losses. What is a company losing $1 million a year worth? Ten times losses? Twenty times losses? You see the point.

With an unprofitable business, the situation becomes about analyzing whether the company can return to profitability, and if so, what the earnings will look like. Then, you can use a proper earnings multiple to estimate value. However, if profitability is not possible, then the liquidation value method is a better way to go.

COMPETITOR'S P/E RATIO

Another way to figure out which earnings multiple to use is to check the P/E ratios of competing companies. Technically, similar companies with similar growth rates should trade at similar valuations. This kind of peer-to-peer comparison is how residential real estate is valued. This method works well during normal times, but not so well during bubbles. For example, all the houses were overvalued during the housing bubble. The same thing can happen with stocks. Just because a slow-growing competitor is trading for 60 times earnings does not mean that you should blindly value your company using such a ridiculous earnings multiple. As always, you have to use your judgment. If the competitors are trading at reasonable valuations, then go ahead and apply similar P/E ratios to your valuations, but make sure that the competitors are actually comparable. No two companies are identical.

ADJUSTING THE "E"

As you know, earnings are the bottom line, which means they are a function of revenues minus expenses. If you simply take the earnings from the income statement without paying attention to how they are derived, you might be using an overstated or understated amount. This will most definitely result in distorted valuations. You have to adjust earnings by removing unusual items from the income statement. This includes unusual or one-time expenses such as restructuring charges, non-cash impairments, goodwill impairments, or non-recurring legal costs. If such expenses appear but are only one-time items, the earnings for that period will be understated. You need to remove them. Also, just like an individual might get a tax refund from the government, a business might report a tax benefit instead of a tax expense. A tax benefit could greatly overstate earnings. Remove it and apply a more appropriate tax expense based on the company's tax rate, which is disclosed in the footnotes. You are doing this so that the "E" for earnings in your valuation estimate is as accurate as possible.

SUMMARY

To value a company based on a particular multiple times earnings is one of the simplest and most widely used techniques. It requires a proper understanding of the earnings component and an educated selection of the earnings multiple. While some investors will tell you that this method of valuation is insufficient, you need to understand it because you will encounter other investors who talk about it and use it. Add this method to your valuation toolbox.

CHAPTER 3

EBITDA and Enterprise Value

A s a buyer, when analyzing the earning power of a business, you would ask the seller about his or her revenues and expenses so that you can understand how they got to the bottom line. If you were interested in acquiring the entire business free and clear, you would not necessarily care about the seller's interest rate on the debt because you would not have the seller's debt. You would arrange your own financing or just pay cash. Also, you might not ask the seller about the tax rate if you were in a completely different tax bracket. Finally, you would definitely not ask about the seller's depreciation or amortization expenses because these are the things you report to the IRS to increase your deductions and pay less in taxes.

Can you imagine an apartment building buyer asking the seller what his depreciation expense was last year? The buyers don't care. They will have their own depreciation deductions when they own the building.

In other words, you would be inquiring about a business's EBITDA, which stands for Earnings Before Interest, Taxes, Depreciation, and Amortization. This is what private equity investors use when valuing businesses. This is also what other companies (public and private) use when evaluating the acquisition of other businesses. They will pay 4 times, 6 times, and even 15 times EBITDA. Obviously, the EBITDA multiple that they are willing to pay will depend on various factors such as the growth rate and stability of the earnings.

The reason you need to care about EBITDA and how it can affect a public company's valuation is that there cannot be a big discrepancy between the valuations of the public versus the private market. If there were, then opportunistic hedge funds would acquire lots of the company's shares on the cheap and turn around and force it to sell out to a private buyer, making a load of money in the process. Such an opportunity would be an arbitrage between the markets.

EBITDA

EBITDA is a non-GAAP financial measure. As you know, the financial statements of public companies have to follow GAAP rules. This means that they include some items that we want excluded, such as depreciation and amortization. Therefore, we need to do some adjustments.

A basic income statement looks like this:

Revenues	$100,000
Cost of goods sold	$60,000
Gross profit	$40,000
Operating expenses:	
Selling, general, and administrative	$20,000
Research and development	$3,000
Depreciation and amortization	$2,000
Operating income	$15,000
Interest expense	$1,000
Income before income taxes	$14,000
Provision for income taxes	$5,000
Net income	$9,000

As you can see, the income statement includes the interest expense, income taxes, depreciation, and amortization. To remove the interest and taxes, simply start with operating income, which in this case is $15,000. Operating income is also called EBIT (Earnings Before Interest and Taxes). Then, add the depreciation and amortization expense back to this amount. In this example, you would add back $2,000 to $15,000 to arrive at $17,000. This is your EBITDA. Some companies provide you with that figure. Also, there are situations when the depreciation and amortization are not shown separately on the income statement because they are combined with other expenses. In that case, you can refer to the cash flow statement to find the correct amount of depreciation and amortization.

Now, the obvious question is which EBITDA multiple to use to value the business. Should the valuation be 4 times EBITDA, 6 times EBITDA, or 10 times EBITDA? To make that determination, remember one thing – its valuation as a private business should not be that much different from what its valuation would be as a public business otherwise, there would be an obvious arbitrage opportunity. Consequently, the EBITDA multiple should have some kind of relationship with the after-tax earnings multiple.

Let's assume that you determined that this business is worth 10 times earnings.

Equity value = $9,000 of net income x 10 = $90,000

What EBITDA multiple do we need to reach the same valuation? Our EBITDA is $17,000. Before we can answer this, we need to determine whether the business has any debt, because the $90,000 valuation is only for the equity portion. The EBITDA valuation is used to calculate the value of the entire business regardless of the capital structure.

Because the interest expense is $1,000, the debt has to be around $20,000. At a 5 percent interest rate, the yearly payment on $20,000 would be nearly $1,000. This is the value of the debt. Therefore, the entire company is worth $110,000, which is $90,000 of equity value plus $20,000 of debt value. Now, we are ready to determine the EBITDA multiple that is needed to make the public and private valuation equal.

$110,000 of total value/$17,000 of EBITDA = 6.47

This is the EBITDA multiple that we need. Let's check the results.

Private Valuation

EBITDA of $17,000 x 6.47 = $110,000

Equity Value = $110,000 of total value - $20,000 of debt = $90,000

Public Valuation

Net income of $9,000 x 10 = $90,000

Equity Value = $90,000

They are the same. Therefore, the EBITDA multiple of 6.47 is equivalent to the earnings multiple of 10.

Some companies have entire business models based on such a relationship. For example, if they know that the public market is valuing their stock at 10 times earnings, then they can issue more shares at 10 times earnings and use the proceeds to make acquisitions of similar private companies at 4 times EBITDA. By doing so, they are building shareholder value. If they made acquisitions at 6.47 times EBITDA, they would not be adding any value. If they made them at 8 times EBITDA, they would be destroying value.

The bottom line is this – the EBITDA multiple has to jive with the earnings multiple. There cannot be a big disconnect between the two. The EBITDA multiple always has to be lower than the earnings multiple because EBITDA has fewer expenses than earnings. The amount of the difference between the two will depend on the expenses that were removed. If the business is extremely capital-light, meaning that it barely has any depreciation expense, and on top of that, it has no debt, then the EBITDA multiple will be close to the earnings multiple because taxes would be the only item removed. However, if the business is extremely capital intensive with a huge depreciation expense and loads of debt, then the difference between the EBITDA multiple and the earnings multiple would be large.

SUM-OF-THE-PARTS

It is not unusual for companies to have more than one business under one entity. The performances of all the individual businesses are consolidated in the financial statements of the parent company. This is why financial statements are referred to as "consolidated financial statements." The problem with presenting the company's financial performance in this way is that you don't know how each individual business is doing. One business might be doing phenomenally well, but another one might be losing money, making the entire parent company look weak. If you estimated the value of a company like this based on its consolidated financial statements, you would have understated its worth. A better way would be to calculate the value of that company by using the sum-of-the-parts method. This means using EBITDA to value the profitable business and finding a liquidation value for the unprofitable business. Often, the parent companies break down the EBITDA figures in the footnotes of the annual reports, so you can use these to calculate the sums.

ENTERPRISE VALUE

As a value investor, when you calculate the value of a business, you want to compare your results with the price that that company is trading for on the open market. Then, you want to buy the stock when your value calculation is higher or at least equal to that price.

In the previous chapter, when you used the earnings multiple to estimate value, you only estimated the value of the equity. Then, all you needed to do was compare your findings with the market cap or stock price.

When using EBITDA to estimate value, you can't just compare it to the market cap or stock price, because you would not be comparing apples to apples. EBITDA allows you to value the entire company regardless of its capital structure. So, in order to make proper comparisons, you have to determine how the public market is currently pricing the company's stock. In other words, you want to find out what it would cost you if you bought up all the common shares and paid off any debt in order to own the entire company free and clear. This is referred to as enterprise value. The name is a bit misleading because it has nothing to do with enterprise value. It should be called enterprise price instead of enterprise value.

Let's imagine that you are buying an apartment building for $1,000,000 and it has a $700,000 mortgage and $300,000 in equity. In order to acquire the property free and clear, you would have to pay $1,000,000 with your money to pay off the $700,000 mortgage and the seller's $300,000 in equity. In this case, the enterprise value (or enterprise price) would equal $1,000,000, which is equity ($300,000) plus debt ($700,000). In stock market terms, the $300,000 in equity that the seller wants would be equivalent to the market capitalization, which is the price per share times the number of shares outstanding. From this example, we can construct a formula for the enterprise value in the following way:

Enterprise Value = Market Value of Equity (Market Capitalization) + Debt

This formula is almost complete, but it is missing one element. Let's use the same example with the apartment property but incorporate cash into it. Imagine that we are buying the same apartment building for $1,000,000 with the same $700,000 mortgage and $300,000 in equity. But this time, in one of the apartment units, you find a briefcase with $200,000 in cash. What is the enterprise value now?

Enterprise Value = Market Value of Equity ($300,000) + Debt ($700,000) - Cash ($200,000) = $800,000

By using the equation above, you can see that the enterprise value is not $1,000,000 anymore. It is now $800,000, because technically, you paid only $800,000 after taking home the briefcase with $200,000. Therefore, the formula has to be adjusted to include EXCESS cash:

Enterprise Value = Market Value of Equity + Debt - Excess Cash

Notice that I said "excess" cash. In our example, the $200,000 is not really needed to operate the apartment building and is therefore considered excess cash. When calculating the enterprise value, some investors use the entire cash balance that they find on the balance sheet. Using all the cash may lead to miscalculations, because assuming that the company does not need to hold any cash to operate its business is not realistic. You want to subtract only the cash that is truly not needed to operate the business. Let me show you what I mean.

Assets	
Current Assets	
Cash	$30,000
Accounts receivable	$3,000
Inventories	$7,000
Prepaid expenses	$1,000
Total current assets	$41,000
Property, plant, and equipment, net	$10,000
Other assets	$2,000
Total assets	$53,000
Liabilities	
Current liabilities	
Accounts payable	$7,000
Accrued expenses	$5,000
Current portion of long-term debt	$2,000
Income taxes payable	$1,000
Total current liabilities	$15,000

This is a partial balance sheet. As you can see, this company has $30,000 in cash. How much of it is excess cash? To determine that, we need look at the current liabilities, which are $15,000. This is the amount that the company will need to satisfy over the next 12 months. To cover this amount, the business will use the current assets, which are $41,000. If we removed $30,000 of cash, the current assets would be $11,000.

$41,000 in current assets - $30,000 in cash = $11,000

This is not enough to cover the $15,000 in current liabilities. Therefore, not all of the $30,000 in cash is excess cash because the business is short by $4,000. The excess cash is $26,000.

$26,000 = $30,000 - $4,000

This is the amount of excess cash that you would subtract when calculating the enterprise value. Then, to determine whether the company is undervalued or overvalued, you would compare the enterprise value (enterprise price) with your estimate of value. This way you would be comparing apples to apples.

If the company had no debt and no excess cash, then the enterprise value would be equal to the market cap.

Enterprise Value = Market Value of Equity + ~~Debt~~ - ~~Excess Cash~~

SUMMARY

EBITDA is a non-GAAP figure that can be used for a quick and easy valuation. This is how private equity values companies. Obviously, the key is to pick a proper EBITDA multiple to reach an accurate valuation. As mentioned before, this multiple should be related to the earnings multiple. Also, it should not be much different from the EBITDA multiples that the market is assigning to similar competing companies. Finally, the thing to remember is that this type of valuation method gives you the value for the entire enterprise, which includes both equity and debt. To make proper value versus price comparisons, you need to calculate the enterprise value, which really should be called the enterprise price.

CHAPTER 4

Free Cash Flow

While both earnings and EBITDA are useful, there are some problems with these metrics. For example, earnings are not equivalent to cash coming into the company because on the income statement, it is a requirement to use accrual accounting, which matches revenues with corresponding costs. EBITDA does not include depreciation and amortization because they are non-cash expenses. However, they are true expenses because in order for depreciation and amortization to be there, the company must have spent some money to acquire some kind of capital equipment in the past.

Because of these problems associated with earnings and EBITDA, some investors turn to another metric to measure the profitability of a company. They use something called free cash flow, which is how much cash the company receives from its operations after spending money on maintaining the firm's productive capacity.

For example, let's say you own an apartment building and you rent it out to tenants. After collecting rent, you have to pay a variety of expenses, such as real estate taxes, utilities, and interest on your mortgage. Whatever is left over is your operating cash flow, but this operating cash flow is not the same as free cash flow because you have one more expenditure to include. Let's say something major breaks that is outside of the regular repairs and maintenance. You have to fix it to maintain your building's productive capacity. If you don't fix it, your renters will leave and you will not receive any more rent. This kind of expense is called a maintenance capital expenditure, also known as maintenance capex. As an apartment owner, you always have to account for maintenance capital expenditures even if nothing breaks because at some point something will break. Examples of maintenance capital expenditures include replacing the apartment building's roof, installing a new heating and air conditioning system, or even purchasing the adjoining lot to expand parking.

After you subtract the maintenance capital expenditures from the operating cash flow, you are left with free cash flow, which you can use for all kinds of purposes, such as investing in your business, paying down debt, paying dividends, buying back shares, or making acquisitions.

The formula for free cash flow is as follows:

Free Cash Flow = Operating Cash Flow - Maintenance Capital Expenditures

Let me show you an example of how you can calculate it. The following is a sample cash flow statement.

Operating Activities		
Net income	$	10,000
Adjustments to reconcile net income to net cash provided by operating activities:		
Depreciation expense		2,000
Gain/loss on sale of fixed assets		100
Changes in operating assets and liabilities:		
Accounts receivable		2,300
Inventories		-1,100
Prepaid expenses and other current assets		110
Accounts payable		1,000
Accrued expenses		950
Income taxes payable		-360
Net cash provided by operating activities	$	15,000
Investing Activities		
Capital expenditures		-5,000
Business acquisitions		-2,000
Purchase/sale of equity investments		1,400
Purchase/sale of short-term investments		-1,100
Net cash used in investing activities	$	-6,700
Financing Activities		
Borrowing/repayment of long-term debt		-3,400
Issuance of common stock		0
Stock repurchases		-2,000
Cash dividends paid		-3,000
Net cash (used in) provided by financing activities	$	-8,400
Net (decrease) increase in cash and cash equivalents		-100
Cash and cash equivalents at beginning of year		4,200
Cash and cash equivalents at end of year	$	4,100

As you can see under the operating activities section of the cash flow statement, net cash provided by operating activities is $15,000. This is the operating cash flow.

The second variable that we have to obtain is capital expenditures. Capital expenditures are found in the investing activities section of the cash flow statement. This line item could be labeled capital expenditures or purchases of property, plant, and equipment. In this case, it is called capital expenditures and it is negative $5,000. It is negative because it is a cash outflow.

Usually companies do not separate capital expenditures into maintenance capital expenditures and growth capital expenditures. You have to estimate them yourself or maybe call the company's CFO and ask how they divide them. Some investors use depreciation as the amount for maintenance capital expenditures. In this case, the depreciation is $2,000 (in the operating activities section), so they would calculate it in the following way.

Free Cash Flow = Operating Cash Flow of $15,000 - Maintenance Capital Expenditures of $2,000 = $13,000

A more accurate way is to refer to the balance sheet. We know that capital expenditures are used to acquire fixed assets, which on the balance sheet are classified as property, plant, and equipment. So, if the balance sheet says that the gross amount for property, plant, and equipment increased from $100,000 to $104,000 from one period to another, we know that $4,000 of capital expenditures was used for growth capital expenditures and $1,000 was used for maintenance capital expenditures ($4,000 + $1,000 = $5,000 on the Cash Flow

Statement). In this case, our free cash flow calculation would be as follows:

Free Cash Flow = Operating Cash Flow of $15,000 - Maintenance Capital Expenditures of $1,000 = $14,000

Once you have the free cash flow number, you can use it to estimate the value of the company's equity or its stock. To keep it simple, you can multiply it times the earnings multiple that you determined previously. Remember, free cash flow is like earnings but more accurate, so using an earnings (not EBITDA) multiple is appropriate.

SUMMARY

Some investors say that net income is a fiction and cash flow is a fact. This is why they prefer to use free cash flow to represent earnings instead of GAAP's net income. This is understandable. You can't pay dividends, make acquisitions, or reduce debt with net income, but you can do all of those things with cash flow. To calculate free cash flow, you only need two variables: operating cash flow, which you obtain from the cash flow statement, and maintenance capital expenditures, which you estimate using both the cash flow statement and balance sheet.

CHAPTER 5

Owners' Earnings

Because earnings metrics have certain drawbacks when it comes to showing a company's cash-generating power, investors turned to free cash flow, which was discussed in the previous chapter. However, free cash flow is not without problems.

During the construction of the cash flow statement, net income is adjusted to arrive at the operating cash flow, which is later used in the calculation of free cash flow. In addition to adjusting net income for non-cash expenses such as depreciation, net income is adjusted for changes in operating assets and liabilities. The changes in operating assets and liabilities are located at the bottom of the operating activities section of the cash flow statement.

Operating Activities

Net income	$	10,000
Adjustments to reconcile net income to net cash provided by operating activities:		
Depreciation expense		2,000
Gain/loss on sale of fixed assets		100
Changes in operating assets and liabilities:		
Accounts receivable		2,300
Inventories		-1,100
Prepaid expenses and other current assets		110
Accounts payable		1,000
Accrued expenses		950
Income taxes payable		-360
Net cash provided by operating activities	$	15,000

Investing Activities

Capital expenditures		-5,000
Business acquisitions		-2,000
Purchase/sale of equity investments		1,400
Purchase/sale of short-term investments		-1,100
Net cash used in investing activities	$	-6,700

Financing Activities

Borrowing/repayment of long-term debt		-3,400
Issuance of common stock		0
Stock repurchases		-2,000
Cash dividends paid		-3,000
Net cash (used in) provided by financing activities	$	-8,400

Net (decrease) increase in cash and cash equivalents		-100
Cash and cash equivalents at beginning of year		4,200
Cash and cash equivalents at end of year	$	4,100

These items come directly from the balance sheet. You can find an explanation of how these changes are calculated in my book, *The Basics of Understanding Financial Statements*.

In this book, all I am going to say is that changes in operating assets and liabilities can overstate or understate a business's cash-generating abilities. For example, if a business suddenly collects a big portion of its accounts receivable, it will show up as a big cash inflow, overstating operating cash flow.

The opposite effect can happen when a business pays off a big portion of its accounts payable, causing a big cash outflow, understating the operating cash flow.

To eliminate the effects of the balance sheet changes, Warren Buffett coined a term called owners' earnings. It is a calculation that is very similar to free cash flow, which was presented in the previous chapter, but without the changes in operating assets and liabilities.

Operating Activities

Net income	$	10,000
Adjustments to reconcile net income to net cash provided by operating activities:		
Depreciation expense		2,000
Gain/loss on sale of fixed assets		100
Changes in operating assets and liabilities:		
Accounts receivable		2,300
Inventories		-1,100
Prepaid expenses and other current assets		110
Accounts payable		1,000
Accrued expenses		950
Income taxes payable		360
Net cash provided by operating activities	$	15,000

Investing Activities

Capital expenditures		-5,000
Business acquisitions		-2,000
Purchase/sale of equity investments		1,400
Purchase/sale of short-term investments		-1,100
Net cash used in investing activities	$	-6,700

Financing Activities

Borrowing/repayment of long-term debt		-3,400
Issuance of common stock		0
Stock repurchases		-2,000
Cash dividends paid		-3,000
Net cash (used in) provided by financing activities	$	-8,400

Net (decrease) increase in cash and cash equivalents		-100
Cash and cash equivalents at beginning of year		4,200
Cash and cash equivalents at end of year	$	4,100

The formula for owners' earnings is:

Owners' Earnings = Adjusted Operating Cash Flow - Maintenance Capital Expenditures

In this example, our adjusted operating cash flow would be calculated in the following way:

	$15,000	
-	$2,300	accounts receivable
+	$1,100	inventories
-	$110	prepaid expenses
-	$1,000	accounts payable
-	$950	accrued expenses
+	$360	income tax payable
	$12,100	

The $12,100 is the adjusted operating cash flow.

Owners' Earnings = $12,100 - $1,000 of maintenance capital expenditures (from the previous chapter) = $11,100

In the last chapter, the calculation of free cash flow was $14,000 and after making some adjustments, the new figure called owners' earnings is $11,100. This is a pretty big difference that will most definitely lead to differences in values. If we used an earnings multiple of 15 to estimate value, here is how the results would differ:

Value = $14,000 of Free Cash Flow x 15 = $210,000

Value = $11,100 of Owners' Earnings x 15 = $166,500

As you can see, the value of equity would be $210,000 based on one cash flow metric and $166,500 based on another cash flow metric. Which one should you use? Both, because some investors use one while others use the other. Also, as with any valuation exercise, you should calculate a value range instead of a single value.

SUMMARY

Owners' earnings is a slightly more accurate metric for calculating a company's cash-flow-generating power. It uses the same variables as the free cash flow formula, but it adjusts the operating cash flow variable by removing changes in operating assets and liabilities. Once the owners' earnings amount has been determined, you can use it to estimate the value of the equity the same way you would use net income.

CHAPTER 6

Discounted Cash Flow Analysis

U p to this point, all of the earnings approaches to value had one thing in common – they relied on one year's worth of earnings or cash flow. Because businesses are living organisms, things change, such as new products being introduced or old products becoming obsolete. How do you value a company that generates $1 million in cash every year for 10 years and then closes its doors? How do you value a company with a pharmaceutical drug that does extremely well under patent protection and then returns to normal afterwards? There is no way to capture such a valuation using the methods we already discussed. We need a more sophisticated method – one that captures cash flows over many years even if those yearly cash flows are drastically different from one another. Therefore, we need the discounted cash flow (DCF) analysis method.

DISCOUNTING AND TIME VALUE OF MONEY

As the name implies, discounted cash flow analysis is about discounting individual cash flows. This means bringing them from the future to the present. This concept is based on the time value of money.

The time value of money is the idea that money available now is worth more than the same amount in the distant future. This is because money on its own has earning power through interest. For example, $1,000 in your savings account can earn you money. So, at the end of one year, this $1,000 will be worth $1,000 plus whatever interest that it earned.

Consequently, $1,000 today is more valuable than $1,000 one year from now. Also, $1,000 today is even more valuable than $1,000 10 years from now. When discounting, you are essentially asking what a particular amount in the future is worth today.

You will receive $1,000 from a relative in five years; what is this worth today? You will receive $1,000 in two years, $5,000 in five years, and $2,000 in 10 years; what is all of it worth today? Answering such questions is what discounted cash flow analysis is all about. Let's answer these two questions.

In order to determine what $1,000 from a relative in five years is worth, we need to pick a discount rate. For right now, don't worry about how the discount rate is determined. Let's say that the discount rate is 10 percent.

$1,000/1.1/1.1/1.1/1.1/1.1 = $621

or

$1,000/(1.1)^5 = $621

So, $1,000 in five years is worth $621 today.

How about $1,000 in two years, $5,000 in five years, and $2,000 in 10 years? This is a bit more complicated because we are dealing with three sums of money to be received at different times. We know one thing for sure; it must be worth less than $8,000, which is the sum of all three. To figure it out, let's discount each sum separately.

- *$1,000/(1.1)^2 = $826*
- *$5,000/(1.1)^5 = $3,105*
- *$2,000/(1.1)^10 = $771*

Total value = $826 + $3,105 + $771 = $4,702

The $4,702 is the answer to the second question, and it is less than $8,000, which is the undiscounted amount.

VALUING A COMPANY

When valuing a company using discounted cash flow analysis, this is exactly what you are doing. You are taking various cash flow amounts from the future and you are bringing them back to the present through discounting. Now, the question becomes, how do you project future cash flows for a company? This is the hard part. Discounted cash flow analysis is powerful. You can use it for any cash flow patterns. The cash flows can be fluctuating, increasing, or decreasing from one year to another. It really doesn't matter, but the problem is forecasting them, which is why discounted cash flow analysis should be used only if you have visibility into the future. This means using it mainly for predictable companies. I am sure you heard the saying "Garbage in, garbage out." Well, this certainly applies to discounted cash flow analysis.

When projecting future cash flows, you essentially have to project separate income statements for five, 10, or however many years you have visibility for. When I say income statement, I don't mean a GAAP income statement. I mean income statements based on cash accounting. You can also call it your version of the cash flow statement.

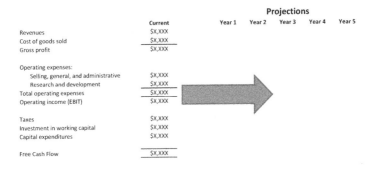

	Current		Projections				
		Year 1	Year 2	Year 3	Year 4	Year 5	
Revenues	$X,XXX						
Cost of goods sold	$X,XXX						
Gross profit	$X,XXX						
Operating expenses:							
Selling, general, and administrative	$X,XXX						
Research and development	$X,XXX						
Total operating expenses	$X,XXX						
Operating income (EBIT)	$X,XXX						
Taxes	$X,XXX						
Investment in working capital	$X,XXX						
Capital expenditures	$X,XXX						
Free Cash Flow	$X,XXX						

REVENUES

Let's start with projecting revenues. This is the hardest and most important part.

- How much are the revenues going to grow?
- What did the management say on the conference calls about revenue growth?
- How fast did revenue grow over the last few years?
- Will past growth continue the same way into the future?
- Is the market big enough to accommodate the projected growth?
- Is the growth coming from an increase in prices or from new products?

- If the market is stable, can the growth come from expanding market share?

Let's assume that based on your research, you project 20 percent revenue growth for the next two years and 15 percent for the following three years. After this period of five years, you assume the company will become mature, so the growth rate will be much lower. This is why we are using five years. Based on these assumptions, the revenue will look like this.

	Current		Year 1	Year 2	Year 3	Year 4	Year 5
					Projections		
Revenues	$100,000		$120,000	$144,000	$165,600	$190,440	$219,006
Cost of goods sold	$X,XXX						
Gross profit	$X,XXX						
Operating expenses:							
Selling, general, and administrative	$X,XXX						
Research and development	$X,XXX						
Total operating expenses	$X,XXX						
Operating income (EBIT)	$X,XXX						
Taxes	$X,XXX						
Investment in working capital	$X,XXX						
Capital expenditures	$X,XXX						
Free Cash Flow	$X,XXX						

COST OF GOODS SOLD

The next step is to figure out the cost of goods sold. Obviously, companies have to sell their products for a price that is higher than the cost to produce them. When they set the price, they might have a rule about how much higher it should be in comparison to the cost, but at the same time, they cannot price it too high because of competition.

- For every dollar in sales, how much does the company spend on the cost of goods sold?
- How much did the company spend on the cost of goods sold in relation to sales over the last five years?
- Is there any reason to believe that this ratio will be different going forward?
- Did the company improve its production process to improve the ratio?
- What did the management say about this ratio in the conference calls?
- Will this ratio improve over time because of operating leverage?

Let's assume that the ratio of the cost of goods sold to sales is 70 percent. However, it keeps decreasing by 1 percent every year until it reaches 65 percent in Year 5.

	Current		Year 1	Year 2	Year 3	Year 4	Year 5
			Projections				
Revenues	$100,000		$120,000	$144,000	$165,600	$190,440	$219,006
Cost of goods sold	$70,000		$82,800	$97,920	$110,952	$125,690	$142,354
Gross profit	$X,XXX						
			69%	68%	67%	66%	65%
Operating expenses:							
Selling, general, and administrative	$X,XXX						
Research and development	$X,XXX						
Total operating expenses	$X,XXX						
Operating income (EBIT)	$X,XXX						
Taxes	$X,XXX						
Investment in working capital	$X,XXX						
Capital expenditures	$X,XXX						
Free Cash Flow	$X,XXX						

GROSS PROFIT

Gross profit is simply the difference between revenues and cost of goods sold.

	Current		Year 1	Year 2	Year 3	Year 4	Year 5
			Projections				
Revenues	$100,000		$120,000	$144,000	$165,600	$190,440	$219,006
Cost of goods sold	$70,000		$82,800	$97,920	$110,952	$125,690	$142,354
Gross profit	$30,000		$37,200	$46,080	$54,648	$64,750	$76,652
Operating expenses:							
Selling, general, and administrative	$X,XXX						
Research and development	$X,XXX						
Total operating expenses	$X,XXX						
Operating income (EBIT)	$X,XXX						
Taxes	$X,XXX						
Investment in working capital	$X,XXX						
Capital expenditures	$X,XXX						
Free Cash Flow	$X,XXX						

OPERATING EXPENSES

As you know, there is a lot more to a business than just making a product for less than its sale price. You have to sell it, which requires paying a salesperson or spending money on advertising.

Then, when you have orders, they have to be filled by someone in the administrative office for which you pay rent. These expenses are not part of the cost of goods sold, because they are not directly related to the making of the product. They are part of selling, general, and administrative (SG&A). You have to estimate them in the future.

- Based on prior years, does the SG&A expense stay in a certain relationship to revenues or gross profit?
- How much of SG&A is variable (ex. sales commissions) and how much of it is fixed?
- Does the management say anything about EBITDA margins going forward?

Let's say that the management estimates that SG&A expenses will rise 10 percent per year for the next five years, which is slower than the revenue growth. This is because some of the SG&A expenses are fixed expenses.

	Current		Year 1	Year 2	Year 3	Year 4	Year 5
		Projections					
Revenues	$100,000		$120,000	$144,000	$165,600	$190,440	$219,006
Cost of goods sold	$70,000		$82,800	$97,920	$110,952	$125,690	$142,354
Gross profit	$30,000		$37,200	$46,080	$54,648	$64,750	$76,652
Operating expenses:							
Selling, general, and administrative	$20,000		$22,000	$24,200	$26,620	$29,282	$32,210
Research and development	$X,XXX						
Total operating expenses	$X,XXX						
Operating income (EBIT)	$X,XXX						
Taxes	$X,XXX						
Investment in working capital	$X,XXX						
Capital expenditures	$X,XXX						
Free Cash Flow	$X,XXX						

The research and development (R&D) expense is very important to many companies because it drives future sales. This is understandable because products need to be improved to keep up with clients' demands and competition.

- What are the management's plans for future R&D expenses?
- Does the company spend a certain percentage of revenues on R&D?

Let's assume that the company spends 7 percent of sales on R&D.

	Current		Projections			
		Year 1	Year 2	Year 3	Year 4	Year 5
Revenues	$100,000	$120,000	$144,000	$165,600	$190,440	$219,006
Cost of goods sold	$70,000	$82,800	$97,920	$110,952	$125,690	$142,354
Gross profit	$30,000	$37,200	$46,080	$54,648	$64,750	$76,652
Operating expenses:						
Selling, general, and administrative	$20,000	$22,000	$24,200	$26,620	$29,282	$32,210
Research and development	$7,000	$8,400	$10,080	$11,592	$13,331	$15,330
Total operating expenses	$X,XXX					
Operating income (EBIT)	$X,XXX					
Taxes	$X,XXX					
Investment in working capital	$X,XXX					
Capital expenditures	$X,XXX					
Free Cash Flow	$X,XXX					

OPERATING INCOME (EBIT)

Based on these projections, we arrive at the following operating income for the next five years.

	Current	Projections				
		Year 1	Year 2	Year 3	Year 4	Year 5
Revenues	$100,000	$120,000	$144,000	$165,600	$190,440	$219,006
Cost of goods sold	$70,000	$82,800	$97,920	$110,952	$125,690	$142,354
Gross profit	$30,000	$37,200	$46,080	$54,648	$64,750	$76,652
Operating expenses:						
Selling, general, and administrative	$20,000	$22,000	$24,200	$26,620	$29,282	$32,210
Research and development	$7,000	$8,400	$10,080	$11,592	$13,331	$15,330
Total operating expenses	$27,000	$30,400	$34,280	$38,212	$42,613	$47,541
Operating income (EBIT)	$3,000	$6,800	$11,800	$16,436	$22,137	$29,111
Taxes	$X,XXX					
Investment in working capital	$X,XXX					
Capital expenditures	$X,XXX					
Free Cash Flow	$X,XXX					

The next step will be estimating taxes. Notice that there is no interest expense anywhere. This is because it is the industry norm to calculate unleveraged free cash flow. The debt will be subtracted from the final estimate of value to arrive at the value of the equity.

TAXES

Estimating taxes is a little bit tricky because taxes are based on net income, which includes all kinds of deductions like depreciation and interest, which we are not including here. One way to estimate them into the future is to calculate the percentage of EBIT that went into paying taxes in the past.

In this example, let's say it is 29 percent.

	Current	Projections				
		Year 1	Year 2	Year 3	Year 4	Year 5
Revenues	$100,000	$120,000	$144,000	$165,600	$190,440	$219,006
Cost of goods sold	$70,000	$82,800	$97,920	$110,952	$125,690	$142,354
Gross profit	$30,000	$37,200	$46,080	$54,648	$64,750	$76,652
Operating expenses:						
Selling, general, and administrative	$20,000	$22,000	$24,200	$26,620	$29,282	$32,210
Research and development	$7,000	$8,400	$10,080	$11,592	$13,331	$15,330
Total operating expenses	$27,000	$30,400	$34,280	$38,212	$42,613	$47,541
Operating income (EBIT)	$3,000	$6,800	$11,800	$16,436	$22,137	$29,111
Taxes	$870	$1,972	$3,422	$4,766	$6,420	$8,442
Investment in working capital	$X,XXX					
Capital expenditures	$X,XXX					
Free Cash Flow	$X,XXX					

INVESTMENT IN WORKING CAPITAL

Every business requires a certain amount of working capital, and as the business grows, the amount of working capital needed must increase. This represents an investment in working capital that has to be accounted for. The formula for working capital is current assets minus current liabilities.

Working Capital = Current Assets - Current Liabilities

You can find both of these figures on the balance sheet. Let's assume the most recent figure for current assets is $25,000 and the most recent figure for current liabilities is $20,000. As a result, working capital is $5,000.

Working Capital = $25,000 - $20,000 = $5,000

Because we said that during the first year, revenues will grow by 20 percent, let's assume that working capital will need to grow by 20 percent as well.

$5,000 x 20% = $1,000

This is what we enter for investment in working capital for Year 1.

After one year, working capital will have grown by 20 percent to $6,000. Because the sales for the second year are also supposed to grow by 20 percent, investment in working capital for Year 2 also needs to grow by the same percentage.

$6,000 x 20% = $1,200

After two years, working capital will have grown to $7,200. Because the sales for the remaining three years are supposed to grow by 15 percent per year, we will grow the working capital investment by this rate as well.

$7,200 x 15% = $1,080

After three years, working capital will have grown to $8,280. The rate of sales growth is still 15 percent per year, so the growth requirement for working capital is also 15 percent for the year.

$8,280 x 15% = $1,242

After four years, working capital will have grown to $9,522. Again, the sales growth is 15 percent, so the growth requirement for working capital is also 15 percent.

$9,522 x 15% = $1,428

This is the amount of investment in working capital that we have projected for Year 5.

	Current	Projections				
		Year 1	Year 2	Year 3	Year 4	Year 5
Revenues	$100,000	$120,000	$144,000	$165,600	$190,440	$219,006
Cost of goods sold	$70,000	$82,800	$97,920	$110,952	$125,690	$142,354
Gross profit	$30,000	$37,200	$46,080	$54,648	$64,750	$76,652
Operating expenses:						
Selling, general, and administrative	$20,000	$22,000	$24,200	$26,620	$29,282	$32,210
Research and development	$7,000	$8,400	$10,080	$11,592	$13,331	$15,330
Total operating expenses	$27,000	$30,400	$34,280	$38,212	$42,613	$47,541
Operating income (EBIT)	$3,000	$6,800	$11,800	$16,436	$22,137	$29,111
Taxes	$870	$1,972	$3,422	$4,766	$6,420	$8,442
Investment in working capital	N/A	$1,000	$1,200	$1,080	$1,242	$1,428
Capital expenditures	$X,XXX					
Free Cash Flow	$X,XXX					

CAPITAL EXPENDITURES

We discussed capital expenditures in previous chapters. If you remember, they consist of growth and maintenance capital expenditures. During the calculation of future free cash flow, you need to include them together instead of separating them into growth and maintenance. This is because the growth capital expenditures are required to generate future sales growth. You can't have your cake and eat it, too. If you do not deduct growth capital expenditures, then you cannot account for as much future growth.

- Are the capital expenditures a certain percentage of revenues?
- Does the management have a certain budget for capital expenditures?

Let's assume that the management stated on the conference calls that the projected capital expenditures would be as follows: $3,000 (Year 1), $5,000 (Year 2), $7,000 (Year 3), $7,000 (Year 4), and $7,000 (Year 5).

	Current	Projections				
		Year 1	Year 2	Year 3	Year 4	Year 5
Revenues	$100,000	$120,000	$144,000	$165,600	$190,440	$219,006
Cost of goods sold	$70,000	$82,800	$97,920	$110,952	$125,690	$142,354
Gross profit	$30,000	$37,200	$46,080	$54,648	$64,750	$76,652
Operating expenses:						
Selling, general, and administrative	$20,000	$22,000	$24,200	$26,620	$29,282	$32,210
Research and development	$7,000	$8,400	$10,080	$11,592	$13,331	$15,330
Total operating expenses	$27,000	$30,400	$34,280	$38,212	$42,613	$47,541
Operating income (EBIT)	$3,000	$6,800	$11,800	$16,436	$22,137	$29,111
Taxes	$870	$1,972	$3,422	$4,766	$6,420	$8,442
Investment in working capital	N/A	$1,000	$1,200	$1,080	$1,242	$1,428
Capital expenditures	$3,000	$3,000	$5,000	$7,000	$7,000	$7,000
Free Cash Flow	$X,XXX					

FREE CASH FLOW

After forecasting and constructing your own version of the cash flow statement, you have derived free cash flow amounts for the next five years.

	Current	Projections				
		Year 1	Year 2	Year 3	Year 4	Year 5
Revenues	$100,000	$120,000	$144,000	$165,600	$190,440	$219,006
Cost of goods sold	$70,000	$82,800	$97,920	$110,952	$125,690	$142,354
Gross profit	$30,000	$37,200	$46,080	$54,648	$64,750	$76,652
Operating expenses:						
Selling, general, and administrative	$20,000	$22,000	$24,200	$26,620	$29,282	$32,210
Research and development	$7,000	$8,400	$10,080	$11,592	$13,331	$15,330
Total operating expenses	$27,000	$30,400	$34,280	$38,212	$42,613	$47,541
Operating income (EBIT)	$3,000	$6,800	$11,800	$16,436	$22,137	$29,111
Taxes	$870	$1,972	$3,422	$4,766	$6,420	$8,442
Investment in working capital	N/A	$1,000	$1,200	$1,080	$1,242	$1,428
Capital expenditures	$3,000	$3,000	$5,000	$7,000	$7,000	$7,000
Free Cash Flow	$X,XXX	$828	$2,178	$3,590	$7,475	$12,241

DISCOUNTING

Now that we have projected future cash flows, we can discount them to the present. Let's discount them one by one using a discount rate of 10 percent.

- *$828 / 1.1 = $753*
- *$2,178 / (1.1) ^ 2 = $1,800*
- *$3,590 / (1.1) ^ 3 = $2,697*
- *$7,475 / (1.1) ^ 4 = $5,106*
- *$12,241 / (1.1) ^ 5 = $7,601*

Total = $753 + $1,800 + $2,697 + $5,106 + $7,601 = $17,956

You can do the discounting of individual cash flows by hand or you can let Excel help you.

	Current	Projections Year 1	Year 2	Year 3	Year 4	Year 5
Revenues	$100,000	$120,000	$144,000	$165,600	$190,440	$219,006
Cost of goods sold	$70,000	$82,800	$97,920	$110,952	$125,690	$142,354
Gross profit	$30,000	$37,200	$46,080	$54,648	$64,750	$76,652
Operating expenses:						
Selling, general, and administrative	$20,000	$22,000	$24,200	$26,620	$29,282	$32,210
Research and development	$7,000	$8,400	$10,080	$11,592	$13,331	$15,330
Total operating expenses	$27,000	$30,400	$34,280	$38,212	$42,613	$47,541
Operating income (EBIT)	$3,000	$6,800	$11,800	$16,436	$22,137	$29,111
Taxes	$870	$1,972	$3,422	$4,766	$6,420	$8,442
Investment in working capital	N/A	$1,000	$1,200	$1,080	$1,242	$1,428
Capital expenditures	$3,000	$3,000	$5,000	$7,000	$7,000	$7,000
Free Cash Flow	$X,XXX	$828	$2,178	$3,590	$7,475	$12,241
Discount Rate	10%					
Discounted Value of Free Cash Flow		$753	$1,800	$2,697	$5,106	$7,601

$17,956

The total value of the discounted cash flows is $17,956. We are done, right? No, we are not. In order to complete the valuation, we have to assume that at the end of five years, the entire company will be sold for cash. This means we have to discount that amount to the present. That discounted amount is called the terminal value.

You have projected that the company's free cash flow will be $12,241 at the end of five years. However, this cash flow amount includes both growth and maintenance capital expenditures. Just like before, we are interested in free cash flow and that has only maintenance capital expenditures, not growth capital expenditures. Let's assume that out of the $7,000 of capital expenditures for that year, $4,000 will be for maintenance and $3,000 will be for growth. So, let's add $3,000 for growth capital expenditures back to our projection of the company's free cash flow, which is $12,241.

$12,241 + $3,000 = $15,241

Because the growth rate beyond the five-year horizon will slow, let's use a conservative multiple of 13 to calculate the terminal value.

$15,241 x 13 = $198,133

This is the amount that the company should sell for in five years. Because this amount is five years in the future, it is worth less today.

$198,133 / (1.1) ^ 5 = $123,026

In summary, the value of the individual cash flows is $17,956 and the terminal value is $123,026. In total, the value of the entire company is $140,982.

	Current	Projections				
		Year 1	Year 2	Year 3	Year 4	Year 5
Revenues	$100,000	$120,000	$144,000	$165,600	$190,440	$219,006
Cost of goods sold	$70,000	$82,800	$97,920	$110,952	$125,690	$142,354
Gross profit	$30,000	$37,200	$46,080	$54,648	$64,750	$76,652
Operating expenses:						
Selling, general, and administrative	$20,000	$22,000	$24,200	$26,620	$29,282	$32,210
Research and development	$7,000	$8,400	$10,080	$11,592	$13,331	$15,330
Total operating expenses	$27,000	$30,400	$34,280	$38,212	$42,613	$47,541
Operating income (EBIT)	$3,000	$6,800	$11,800	$16,436	$22,137	$29,111
Taxes	$870	$1,972	$3,422	$4,766	$6,420	$8,442
Investment in working capital	N/A	$1,000	$1,200	$1,080	$1,242	$1,428
Capital expenditures	$3,000	$3,000	$5,000	$7,000	$7,000	$7,000
Free Cash Flow	$X,XXX	$828	$2,178	$3,590	$7,475	$12,241
Discount Rate	10%					
Discounted Value of Free Cash Flow		$753	$1,800	$2,697	$5,106	$7,601

$17,956

Year 5 Free Cash Flow	$12,241
Growth CAPEX	$3,000
Terminal Adjusted Free Cash Flow	$15,241
Terminal Multiple	13
Undiscounted Terminal Value	$198,135
Discounted Terminal Value	$123,026

$123,026 $140,982

EQUITY VALUE

Because the free cash flow figures we calculated were unlevered, meaning that they did not include the interest payments, the total value calculated represents the value of the entire enterprise. As stock market investors, we are interested in the value of equity and individual shares. To calculate the equity value, simply subtract the net debt. Then, if you want the value of each share, divide the equity value by the diluted number of shares.

- *Company Value = $140,982*
- *Debt = $30,000*
- *Equity Value = $140,982 - $30,000 = $110,982*
- *Number of shares = 10,000*
- *Value of each share = $110,982 / 10,000 = $11.10*

DISCOUNT RATE

Discounted Cash Flow analysis requires a lot of assumptions and forecasts. One assumption is the discount rate, which up to this point was 10 percent. I just used 10 percent for simplicity, but in this section, we will talk about how to choose an appropriate rate. The reason a discount rate is important is that it can dramatically change the valuation of a company.

To determine a discount rate, you can go about it the easy way or the complicated way. The easy way is to treat the discount rate as your own required rate of return. What kind of return do you require per year to consider an investment? I like to think of a range between 7 and 13 percent. If the company is super predictable and stable, I will go with 7 percent. Many blue-chip companies would qualify. However, if the company were less predictable, smaller, and riskier, I would go with 13 percent. You can go even higher. It is your call. When valuing companies, I like to play with the discount rate. I will go with 10 percent and see what value I get. Then, I will change it around and record the changes in value. If the company is trading for $500 million, but my valuation range is between $1 billion and $4 billion, then it doesn't really matter if I nail the discount rate. Either way, the stock is cheap. But if the valuation range is between $300 million and $1 billion, then I had better narrow down my discount rate, so it is more precise.

The complicated way to determine the discount rate is by using the weighted average cost of capital (WACC). As you know, the company's assets are financed by either debt or equity. Both of these capital sources have costs associated with them. While implicit, equity investors want to put their money where they can receive the highest return possible for a specific risk level. If they aren't going to get that return on a potential investment, they will not buy it, and if they haven't gotten it from a current investment in their expected time frame, they will sell. Debt investors also want a return, but this return requirement is more explicit in the form of an interest rate. By using WACC, you are essentially trying to calculate the average cost of capital between the equity and debt.

Step 1: Determine Capital Structure

- How is the company financed?
- Is it 100 percent equity?
- Is it 50 percent equity and 50 percent debt?

The enterprise value is the market value of the equity plus the market value of the debt. The market value of the equity is the market capitalization. If the company's issued bonds are publicly traded, you can look up the market price, but if the bonds are not publicly traded, then you have to use the total debt amount from the balance sheet.

Let's assume the market cap is $70,000 and the amount, or market value, of the debt is $30,000. The total capitalization is $100,000.

The equity represents 70 percent of the total capitalization and the debt represents the remaining 30 percent. So, the WACC formula will be as follows:

WACC = (70% x Cost of Equity) + (30% x After-Tax Cost of Debt)

Step 2: Determine After-Tax Cost of Debt

Let's start with the debt side because it is more straightforward. The cost of debt is what the company pays in interest. Look it up in the footnotes. Let's assume it is 5 percent. Because interest is tax deductible, we are interested in the after-tax cost of debt. Let's assume a 35 percent tax rate.

5% x (1 - 35% tax rate) = 3.25 %

This is the after-tax cost of debt. Let's plug it into the formula.

WACC = (70% x Cost of Equity) + (30% x 3.25%)

Step 3: Determine the Cost of Equity

Determining the cost of equity is trickier because it is not explicit. Unlike debt investors, equity investors do not have a written agreement for a certain rate of return. However, just because there is no agreement does not mean there is no cost. The most common method of calculating the cost of equity is the capital asset pricing model (CAPM), which compensates investors in two ways: through the time value of money and risk. The time value of money is represented by a risk-free rate while the risk is represented by an equity market risk premium and beta.

Cost of Equity = Risk Free Rate + Equity Market Risk Premium x Beta

A risk-free rate is the interest rate that you can yield by investing in government bonds. You can look up the current five-year U.S. government bond rate on the Federal Reserve website. I am using a five-year projection model in the DCF analysis, and for this example, I will use 1.50 percent.

The equity market risk premium is the extra return that investors expect to get over the risk-free rate of U.S. Treasury bills in order to invest in the stock market. It is defined as:

Equity Market Risk Premium = (Expected Market Return - Risk Free Rate)

Let's use 10 percent as the expected market return. You can use any number, but over several years, this is how much the market usually returns per year.

Equity Market Risk Premium = 10.00% - 1.50% = 8.50%

Beta is the risk of an individual stock based on its volatility in relation to the volatility of the market as a whole. A stock with a beta of one means that the stock's price moves exactly with the overall market. A stock with a beta of more than one means that the stock is more volatile than the overall market, and a stock with a beta of less than one means the stock is less volatile than the market. You can find your stock's beta at Morningstar.com under the basic quote information. Let's assume that in our example, the beta is 1.66.

Let's plug in all the variables to calculate the cost of equity.

Cost of Equity = Risk-Free Rate + Equity Market Risk Premium x Beta

Cost of Equity = 1.5% + (8.5% x 1.66) = 15.61%

Step 4: Finish Calculating WACC

WACC = (70% x 15.61%) + (30% x 3.25%) = 11.90%, rounded to 12%.

This is the discount rate that you would use in your DCF analysis if you chose to determine the discount rate using WACC.

SUMMARY

As you can see, the discounted cash flow analysis is a more complex valuation technique. It accounts for cash flows from many different years and it brings their value to the present. With it, you can value any cash flow stream, but the obvious problem is being able to accurately forecast and predict. If you make incorrect assumptions, you will get an incorrect valuation. Because the input data is so sensitive, it is common for stock analysts to reach different valuations of the same companies.

CHAPTER 7

Dividend Discount Model

T he discounted cash flow analysis is a method that uses unlevered cash flow to estimate the value of an entire company regardless of its capital structure. You did not have to include the interest on debt. The dividend discount model is a similar valuation technique, but instead of valuing the entire company, it values an individual share by discounting future dividend payments and the terminal value of that share.

The dividend discount model is one of the oldest valuation techniques. As the name implies, it is about dividends, so the company needs to be paying dividends. This includes mainly mature companies that return cash to shareholders in the form of dividends. This model is not suitable for high-growth companies with no dividends. For such companies, the discounted cash flow analysis is more suitable, assuming, of course, that you can forecast future cash flows. Let's do a valuation example.

Let's assume we are valuing a company that has current earnings per share of $3.50 with a dividend payout of 30 percent. This means that dividends per share are $1.05.

VARIABLES

FACTS

Current Earning Per Share	$3.50
Current Dividend Per Share	$1.05
Dividend Payout	30%

Because the company is a dividend aristocrat, which means it has paid and increased dividends for the past 25 years, we can rely on its historical earnings and dividend growth to project the future. Consequently, we estimate that the company will grow earnings per share at 12 percent for the next five years and 9 percent for the following five years. We will keep the dividend payout at 30 percent. The discount rate that we will choose is 8 percent. For the P/E ratio in 10 years, we will use 13. This will be used to calculate the terminal value.

ASSUMPTIONS

Earnings Growth Rate (1st Five Years)	12.0%
Earnings Growth Rate (2nd Five Years)	9.0%
Discount Rate	8.0%
P/E Ratio in 10 Years	13

Based on these inputs, we get the following results.

VARIABLES

FACTS	
Current Earning Per Share	$3.50
Current Dividend Per Share	$1.05
Dividend Payout	30%

ASSUMPTIONS	
Earnings Growth Rate (1st Five Years)	12.0%
Earnings Growth Rate (2nd Five Years)	9.0%
Discount Rate	8.0%
P/E Ratio in 10 Years	13

RESULTS	
Value of Future Dividends Today	$12.34
Value of Future Sales Price Today	$57.15
Value of the Stock	$69.48

VALUE CALCULATIONS

Year	Projected Earnings	Payout Ratio	Dividends	Discounted Dividends
1	$3.92	30%	$1.18	$1.09
2	$4.39	30%	$1.32	$1.13
3	$4.92	30%	$1.48	$1.17
4	$5.51	30%	$1.65	$1.21
5	$6.17	30%	$1.85	$1.26
6	$6.72	30%	$2.02	$1.27
7	$7.33	30%	$2.20	$1.28
8	$7.99	30%	$2.40	$1.29
9	$8.71	30%	$2.61	$1.31
10	$9.49	30%	$2.85	$1.32
				$12.34

	Projected Earnings	P/E Ratio in 10 Years	Terminal Value	Discounted Terminal Value
10	$9.49	13	$123.38	$57.15

Projected earnings per share are shown in the second column under the value calculations heading. As you can see, the dividend payout ratio stays at 30 percent under the payout ratio column. This translates into individual dividends in the fourth column. The fifth column shows discounted dividends, which represent the values of the individual future dividends today. The total value of the discounted dividends is $12.34, which is the sum of the fifth column.

Finally, in Year 10, the company will have earnings per share of $9.49. At an earnings multiple of 13, the terminal price will be $123.38 per share.

Because this amount is in 10 years, it has to be discounted to the present using an 8 percent discount rate. The discounted terminal value of the stock is $57.15.

The stock is worth $69.48, which is equal to the value of the future dividends, $12.34, plus the value of the future sales price, $57.15. Once you know the value, you can easily compare it to the stock price to decide if the stock is undervalued or overvalued.

SUMMARY

The dividend discount model is based on the same philosophy as the discounted cash flow analysis model. The only difference is the items that are being discounted. Under the dividend discount model, individual dividend payments are being discounted to arrive at the value of an individual share. Under the discounted cash flow analysis, unlevered cash flows are being discounted to arrive at the value of the entire company. Also, for both methods, a terminal value is estimated and discounted to the present.

CHAPTER 8

Conclusion

I n this book, I presented you with several different ways to value companies. One method might work well for one company while another method might work better for another company. This is where you have to use your judgment to decide which ones to use when.

While some investors would love to be able to calculate a company's value to exact precision, this is simply not possible. Too many unknowns go into estimating value. Instead of searching for the impossible, use a few different valuation techniques at the same time. Calculate value ranges based on different assumptions. Then, compare the stock price to your findings. If you are unsure about whether the stock is undervalued, then simply don't buy. Only invest when the discrepancy between price and value is obvious. Don't be tempted to change the assumptions to arrive at a value that will make the stock look undervalued. This is especially true when it comes to the discounted cash flow analysis, where you can manipulate the numbers until you get the value that you want.

I hope that this book helped you understand how to value a company. The more you do it, the better you will get. Also, the more you know about the business, the easier it will be to value it because making accurate assumptions becomes possible.

Also, I encourage you to watch my video, *How to Value a Company*, at classicvalueinvestors.com under the Value Investing University section.

CHAPTER 9

Other Books by the Author

- *Why Are We So Clueless about the Stock Market?*
- *The Basics of Understanding Financial Statements*
- *100 Ways to Find Investment Ideas*
- *Gold Production from Beginning to End*
- *How Gold Companies Finance Themselves*
- *Due Diligence: How to Research a Stock*
- *Scuttlebutt Investor*
- *Investment Wisdom*
- *How to Profit from the Coronavirus Recession*

Made in the USA
Monee, IL
01 September 2020